POPULAR SONGS

HAL LEONARD
STUDENT PIANO LIBRARY

Sounds Of Christmas
Volume 3
Seasonal Songs for Two

Arranged by Rosemary Barrett Byers

T0087812

CONTENTS

Edited by J. Mark Baker

ISBN 1-4234-0242-1

HAL•LEONARD®
CORPORATION

7777 W. BLUEMOUND RD. P.O. BOX 13819 MILWAUKEE, WI 53213

Visit Hal Leonard Online at
www.halleonard.com

Blue Christmas

Words and Music by Billy Hayes
and Jay Johnson
Arranged by Rosemary Barrett Byers

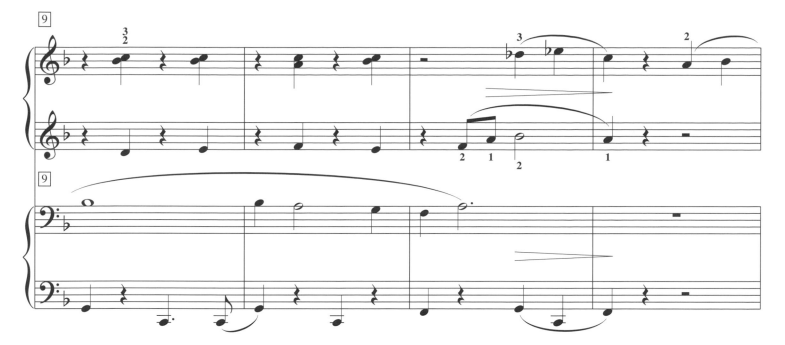

3

(1'35")

4

Christmas Is A-Comin'

(May God Bless You)

Words and Music by Frank Luther
Arranged by Rosemary Barrett Byers

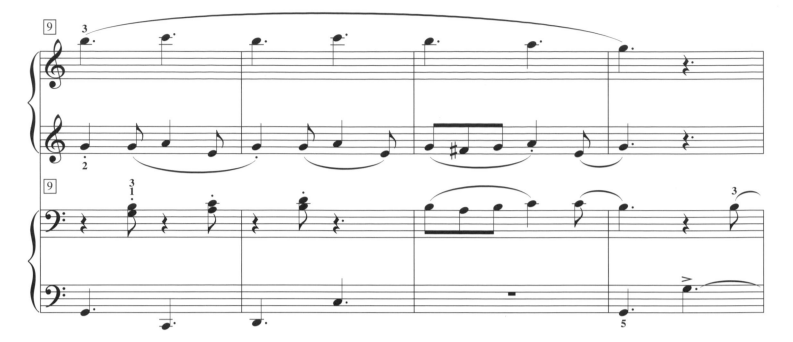

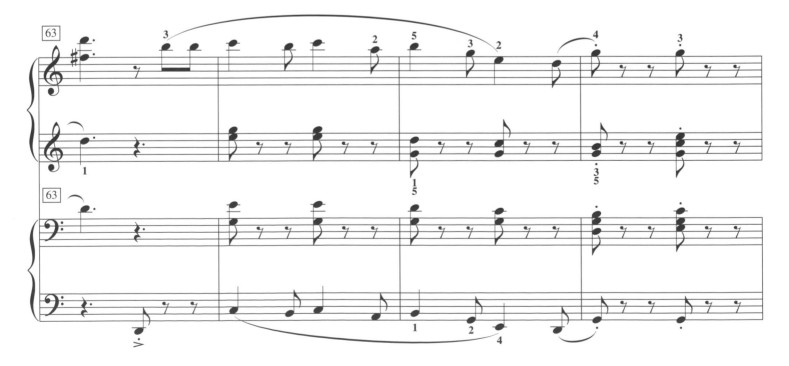

(1'32")

I Saw Mommy Kissing Santa Claus

Words and Music by Tommie Connor
Arranged by Rosemary Barrett Byers

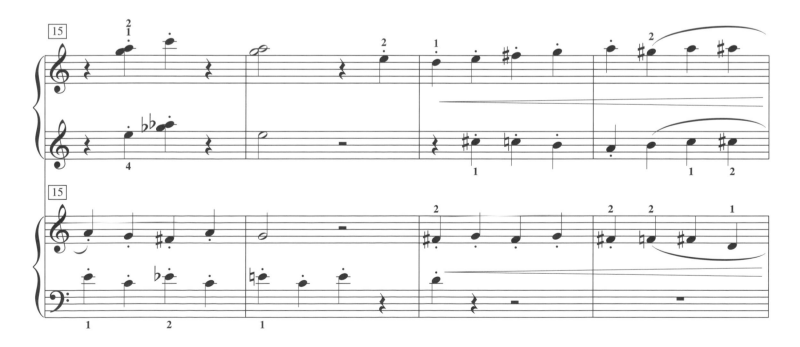

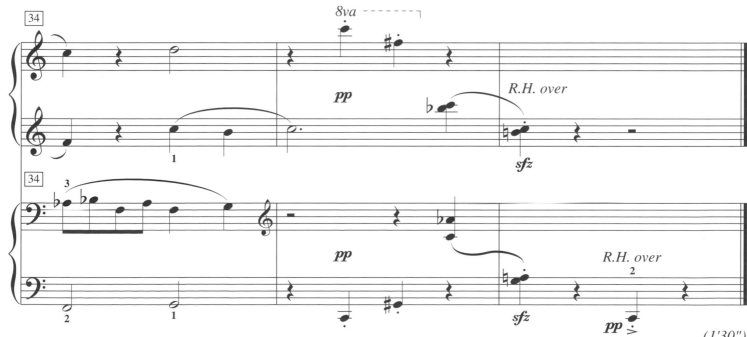

(1'30")

Merry Christmas, Darling

Words and Music by Richard Carpenter
and Frank Pooler
Arranged by Rosemary Barrett Byers

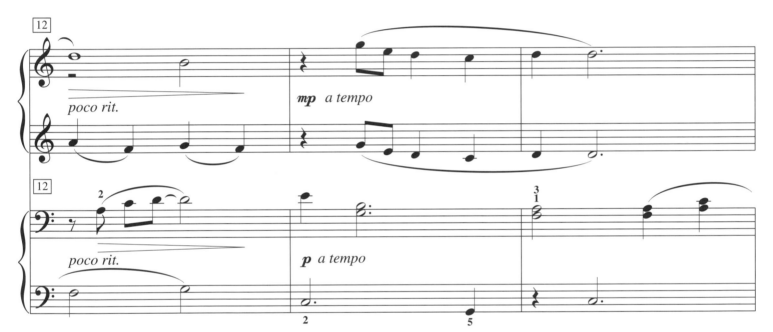

19

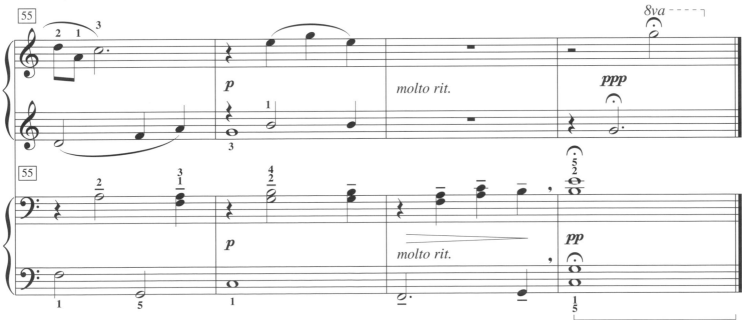

(2'50")

Silver Bells

from the Paramount Picture THE LEMON DROP KID

Words and Music by Jay Livingston
and Ray Evans
Arranged by Rosemary Barrett Byers

(2'32")

Shake Me I Rattle

(Squeeze Me I Cry)

Words and Music by Hal Hackady
and Charles Naylor
Arranged by Rosemary Barrett Byers

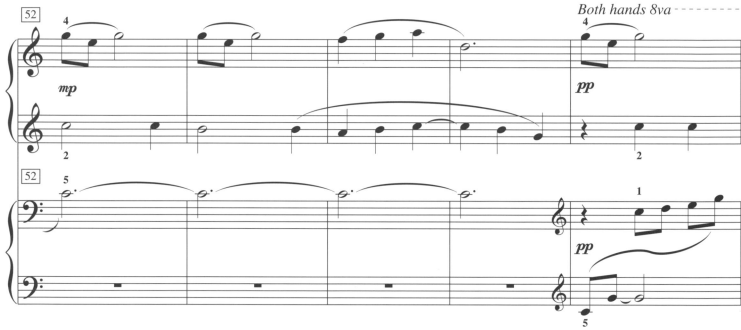

(2'05")